authentic living

jesus every day

Devotional Guide

CANDACE | *DaySpring*

candacecbure.com | dayspring.com

WELCOME!

I am so excited about this book you're holding! It's been a dream of mine to create a study guide to help people understand the Bible, find Jesus, and grow in their faith. The Bible has been such an influential book for me personally, and choosing to put my faith in Jesus has made all the difference in my life.

Caution: this is not a wishy-washy self-improvement book or a 10-step self-help guide. The entries in this book are designed to help you discover how personally following Jesus is the best decision you can make. As you go through this study guide, I hope you will choose to believe what the Bible teaches and put your trust in Jesus for salvation. You won't regret it—I promise!

On this journey, let your mind go there, let it discover the new ways God is speaking to you, open yourself to the process and you are sure to find the answers to living your best, authentic life.

In this together, *Candace*

Before You Get Started on This Adventure

*H*ere's the deal. You're picking this book up and are either super excited to dig in or wondering if you really want to start this journey with me. I get it. Trust me, I do. And while I can tell you that this study can undoubtedly change your life, you may not be eager to jump in based on my enthusiasm alone. But would you do me a favor? Would you at least read through this first section before you put this book back on the shelf?

Before jumping into it, you might be wondering why the Bible is worth reading or what all the talk about being "saved" means. You may feel like you'll never measure up to God's standards—that there's no hope for you—so why even try? Or maybe you feel like you're doing just fine and life is actually pretty good, so why would you need to dig deep into God's Word?

Wherever you are in your spiritual journey, I want you to know you're not alone. In this first section, I've answered some questions people typically ask me about my Christian faith. I hope these answers will be helpful to you too.

Why should I read and study the Bible?

The world is full of all kinds of books that tell stories, teach concepts, inspire, and entertain. Heck, I've even written a few of them! Many books have influenced the world throughout history, but none compare with the Bible.

We all love a good story, right? While the Bible is full of history, wisdom, guidelines, and poetry, it's actually the epic story about all of creation and time from the beginning to the end. In the Bible, God is the ultimate storyteller—He shares His plan, His story, and His design for the world and for humanity.

The story begins with God creating His beloved humanity—Adam and Eve—in His image. But they destroyed their relationship with Him by choosing power instead of trusting in Him. Then the rest of the Bible—the greatest love story ever told—continues as God sets His plan in motion to bring His people back to Himself.

While there are other books that claim to be "holy," and even some that may contain useful ideas or wise words, no other book explains so clearly humanity's desperate need for rescue and how God Himself came to the rescue by sending His only Son, Jesus. No other book is so transformational because no other book shows us how much we are *loved* by our Creator.

What does it mean to be "saved"?

When followers of Jesus talk about being saved, we mean that Jesus rescued us from the ultimate consequence of sin—eternal separation from God—and our lives are no longer controlled by sin or filled with darkness, hopelessness, shame, guilt, and fear. Jesus shines His light, freedom, joy, peace, and hope into our lives.

God doesn't want sin to have any control over us. He wants to have a relationship with us. He wants us to live full, abundant, joyful lives that reflect His goodness back to others! That's why Jesus came—to save us from the punishment we deserve because of our sin and to give us new life. We all deserve God's judgment. Because He is holy, He cannot allow sin anywhere near Him. Because of sin, we cannot earn our way to having a relationship with God. But He loves us so much that He sent Jesus to take the punishment for us. He wants to spend eternity with us. No matter how far we've fallen, no matter what we've done, Jesus loves us and wants to save us.

Being saved doesn't mean we are spared from all suffering in our lives. But it does mean we have God's presence with us and the promise of spending forever with Him—an eternity free from all pain and suffering. Does it sound too good to be true? It's not! Jesus is ready to save us the moment we open our hearts to Him and accept His unconditional love for us.

*A*fter reading the first two questions and reflecting on them, do you feel like this book isn't for you or you can't relate? If so, please promise me that you'll keeping reading—because I've written this section just for you!

What if I don't need to be "saved"?

I get this too—you're a good person, you help others, you live honestly, you probably donate time and money to charity, and you're not hurting anyone. Why do you need to be "saved"? You're good, right? Compared to others, you're practically a saint!

But we have to realize that God's standards are different from human standards. If we just compare ourselves to other people, it's easy to think we're good enough. But when we compare ourselves to God's standards, we fall miserably short. Every. Single. Time.

Take, for example, the Ten Commandments. I'm pretty sure that before I was even two years old I broke several of them. I probably lied about a cookie I had stolen (commandments 7 and 8), dishonored and disobeyed my parents (commandment 4), and deeply coveted my friend's baby doll (commandment 10).

So what's my point? Just like Adam and Eve, we have *all* fallen short of God's standards. Our sin separates us from our Creator. God says that if we break even one commandment, it's as if we're guilty of breaking them all. There isn't one of us who can say we are sinless. And doing good things to earn God's approval doesn't erase our sinfulness either.

But because God loves us, He sent His Son, Jesus, to die so that all people—the bad, the good, and everyone in between—could have a relationship with Him.

Is there really only one way to God?

This is a tough one for a lot of people, but the short answer is *yes*. There is only one way to God, and it's through Jesus Christ. Jesus said, "I am the way and the truth and the life. No one comes to the Father except through Me" (John 14:6 NIV). Jesus didn't say, "I am one of the ways to God." He's *it*—He's the *only* way.

Though this idea may seem very narrow, it's actually comforting. Many religions teach people to work to earn their right standing with God. With Jesus, being right with God doesn't depend on what we do or don't do; it depends on what Jesus has already done: He died on the cross to take the punishment for our sins and then rose again to give us life with Him. All we have to do is acknowledge our sinfulness, ask God for His forgiveness, and then humbly accept His gift of salvation. Then we get to spend our lives loving and following Him. Isn't that the best news ever?

Why is Jesus the only way to God? Because He is the *only* perfect person to ever walk this planet. Jesus is also God's only Son (John 3:16) and "the image of the invisible God" (Colossians 1:15 NIV). Jesus—the living God—died and rose again so we could have a relationship with God! No other person can be described in this way.

Friend, I promise that if you ask God how to find Him, He will make it very clear to you, and it will be the greatest adventure of your life!

Jesus said, "I am the way and the truth and the life."

$\mathcal{B}$ecause I believe the Bible shows us who Jesus is and how we can have a relationship with Him, I want to help you get to know Him too. That's what this study guide is all about.

How do I use this study guide?

Here's how it works: each day has a reading from the Bible and then some questions to help you think about and apply the biblical concepts. It's that simple! There's no "right" answer, and you can add your own questions and thoughts at any point, on any page.

I can't stress this enough: get in the *zone*. The zone is where you are distraction-free and able to listen as God speaks to you through the Bible. I get a lot more out of studying the Bible when I'm in the zone. You don't have to be in a quiet place or alone. You can get in the zone with friends who are hungry for learning more about the Bible and how to live.

Ideally, this is a personal journey where God will speak directly to your heart. But going through the study with friends can bring you encouragement and help you connect with others in really valuable ways. If you'd like, you could complete a day's study alone and then come together with a group of friends to discuss what God is showing you. You decide!

Do I need to use a Bible?

If you don't have a Bible, no worries. We have printed the text for you here. But I'd encourage you to get a Bible of your own. Translation? While there are many to pick from, Bible translations that use up-to-date English—such as the CSB, ESV, and NIV—make the Bible more relatable and easier for me to understand.

The Bible readings in this study are taken from several different translations, so take note. Maybe you'll discover you like one more than the others after reading through the passages from the Bible in this book.

You can use this workbook alongside your Bible. Open your Bible up, read it, highlight it, circle stuff, ask God to speak to your heart, and then *just listen*. You can also dig deeper beyond just the reading for the day. Feel free to chase a rabbit trail in the Word (also known as the Bible)—you never know where it will lead! But if you are a little intimidated by all that, I designed this study so you can just read the entry for the day and answer the questions. Simple!

Ask God to speak to your heart.

Let's do this!

As you go through each day's study, pray through it. Don't just complete it so you can check it off your to-do list. And don't look to me to tell you the answers or what to think; look to the Word and ask God to speak to you.

How do you know when God is speaking to you? God speaks to us in different ways, and He'll never say something that contradicts what the Bible teaches. When I'm reading certain verses and my heart does something like a flip-flop, I know in that moment that the Holy Spirit is showing me something important and I need to pay attention.

God will also speak to us through friends, pastors, and teachers. He may even reveal Himself to us through nature or certain circumstances. Just be open to however He wants to speak to you.

Lastly, don't be afraid. The most repeated command in the Bible is "Do not fear," and one of the most common promises from God is "I am with you." So jump into this adventure and ask God what He wants to reveal to you. Whether you are new to the Bible or super familiar with it, I can tell you this: God's Word is living and active. It will bring you life, and you will thrive every day as you find truth, peace, and hope within its pages. Let's go!

Before you begin, what questions do you have about the Bible, salvation, prayer, heaven, or starting a relationship with Jesus? If you'd like, you can pray right now and ask God to help you find answers to these questions.

_____
_____
_____
_____
_____
_____
_____
_____
_____
_____
_____
_____
_____
_____
_____
_____
_____
_____

If you'd like to learn more about the Bible or
what it means to follow Jesus, please visit

www.candacecbure.com

Seeking God First

DEUTERONOMY 6:1—9 (CSB)

"This is the command—the statutes and ordinances—the LORD your God has commanded me to teach you, so that you may follow them in the land you are about to enter and possess. Do this so that you may fear the LORD your God all the days of your life by keeping all His statutes and commands I am giving you, your son, and your grandson, and so that you may have a long life. Listen, Israel, and be careful to follow them, so that you may prosper and multiply greatly, because the LORD, the God of your fathers, has promised you a land flowing with milk and honey.

"Listen, Israel: The LORD our God, the LORD is one. Love the LORD your God with all your heart, with all your soul, and with all your strength. These words that I am giving you today are to be in your heart. Repeat them to your children. Talk about them when you sit in your house and when you walk along the road, when you lie down and when you get up. Bind them as a sign on your hand and let them be a symbol on your forehead. Write them on the doorposts of your house and on your city gates."

What are your priorities in life?

Why do you think God wants to be first in our lives?

What might be some benefits of obeying and following God?

SEEKING GOD FIRST CONFIRMS OUR *dependence on Him.*

What are some practical steps you can take to seek God first in your life?

_____
_____
_____
_____
_____
_____
_____
_____
_____
_____
_____
_____
_____
_____
_____

Your Biggest Takeaway

Living Courageously

Joshua 1:1–9 (NIV)

After the death of Moses the servant of the LORD, the LORD said to Joshua son of Nun, Moses' aide: "Moses My servant is dead. Now then, you and all these people, get ready to cross the Jordan River into the land I am about to give to them—to the Israelites. I will give you every place where you set your foot, as I promised Moses. Your territory will extend from the desert to Lebanon, and from the great river, the Euphrates—all the Hittite country—to the Mediterranean Sea in the west. No one will be able to stand against you all the days of your life. As I was with Moses, so I will be with you; I will never leave you nor forsake you. Be strong and courageous, because you will lead these people to inherit the land I swore to their ancestors to give them. Be strong and very courageous. Be careful to obey all the law My servant Moses gave you; do not turn from it to the right or to the left, that you may be successful wherever you go. Keep this Book of the Law always on your lips; meditate on it day and night, so that you may be careful to do everything written in it. Then you will be prosperous and successful. Have I not commanded you? Be strong and courageous. Do not be afraid; do not be discouraged, for the LORD your God will be with you wherever you go."

When you face an unexpected or difficult situation, how do you typically respond?

In these verses, what are some of the promises God gave to Joshua and the Israelites?

What can you learn about fear and courage from God's words to Joshua?

COURAGE DOESN'T MEAN YOU DON'T GET AFRAID. COURAGE MEANS YOU *don't let fear stop you.*

— BETHANY HAMILTON

In what areas of your life do you want to live more courageously?

_____

_____

_____

_____

_____

_____

_____

_____

_____

_____

_____

_____

_____

_____

_____

_____

Your Biggest Takeaway

Kindness Always Wins

ROMANS 12:2–8 (NLT)

Don't copy the behavior and customs of this world, but let God transform you into a new person by changing the way you think. Then you will learn to know God's will for you, which is good and pleasing and perfect.

Because of the privilege and authority God has given me, I give each of you this warning: Don't think you are better than you really are. Be honest in your evaluation of yourselves, measuring yourselves by the faith God has given us. Just as our bodies have many parts and each part has a special function, so it is with Christ's body. We are many parts of one body, and we all belong to each other.

In His grace, God has given us different gifts for doing certain things well. So if God has given you the ability to prophesy, speak out with as much faith as God has given you. If your gift is serving others, serve them well. If you are a teacher, teach well. If your gift is to encourage others, be encouraging. If it is giving, give generously. If God has given you leadership ability, take the responsibility seriously. And if you have a gift for showing kindness to others, do it gladly.

In the past week, how have you shown or received kindness?

How might showing kindness to other people help us to not think too highly of ourselves?

Who are people in your life who have the gift of serving others with kindness?

What do they do that makes those gifts evident?

KINDNESS IS BEING
A BREATH OF
fresh air
TO SOMEONE ELSE
WHEN THEY FEEL
LIKE THEY ARE
suffocating.
— UNKNOWN

In what ways this week can you respond in kindness even when others are unkind?

_____

_____

_____

_____

_____

_____

_____

_____

_____

_____

_____

_____

_____

_____

A Note From Candace

We don't have to be like the world around us. We can be different and make a difference. How? Practice kindness—daily. I have found that even the smallest act of kindness can make a big impact.

DAY 4

Love Never Fails

I Corinthians 13 (NIV)

If I speak in the tongues of men or of angels, but do not have love, I am only a resounding gong or a clanging cymbal. If I have the gift of prophecy and can fathom all mysteries and all knowledge, and if I have a faith that can move mountains, but do not have love, I am nothing. If I give all I possess to the poor and give over my body to hardship that I may boast, but do not have love, I gain nothing.

Love is patient, love is kind. It does not envy, it does not boast, it is not proud. It does not dishonor others, it is not self-seeking, it is not easily angered, it keeps no record of wrongs. Love does not delight in evil but rejoices with the truth. It always protects, always trusts, always hopes, always perseveres.

Love never fails. But where there are prophecies, they will cease; where there are tongues, they will be stilled; where there is knowledge, it will pass away. For we know in part and we prophesy in part, but when completeness comes, what is in part disappears. When I was a child, I talked like a child, I thought like a child, I reasoned like a child. When I became a man, I put the ways of childhood behind me. For now we see only a reflection as in a mirror; then we shall see face to face. Now I know in part; then I shall know fully, even as I am fully known.

And now these three remain: faith, hope and love. But the greatest of these is love.

When have you experienced unfailing love?

Which of the attributes listed in I Corinthians 13 is the most meaningful to you?

Why do you suppose God said that love is greater than faith and hope?

TRUST IN GOD'S

unfailing love.

In what ways might you be able to better love those who are difficult to love?

_____

_____

_____

_____

_____

_____

_____

_____

_____

_____

_____

_____

_____

_____

_____

Your Biggest Takeaway

Growing with Others

ACTS 2:42–47; 4:32–37 (CSB)

They devoted themselves to the apostles' teaching, to the fellowship, to the breaking of bread, and to prayer.

Everyone was filled with awe, and many wonders and signs were being performed through the apostles. Now all the believers were together and held all things in common. They sold their possessions and property and distributed the proceeds to all, as any had need. Every day they devoted themselves to meeting together in the temple, and broke bread from house to house. They ate their food with joyful and sincere hearts, praising God and enjoying the favor of all the people. Every day the Lord added to their number those who were being saved. . . .

Now the entire group of those who believed were of one heart and mind, and no one claimed that any of his possessions was his own, but instead they held everything in common. With great power the apostles were giving testimony to the resurrection of the Lord Jesus, and great grace was on all of them. For there was not a needy person among them because all those who owned lands or houses sold them, brought the proceeds of what was sold, and laid them at the apostles' feet. This was then distributed to each person as any had need.

Joseph, a Levite from Cyprus by birth, the one the apostles called Barnabas (which is translated Son of Encouragement), sold a field he owned, brought the money, and laid it at the apostles' feet.

Who or what strengthens you the most in your life?

In the verses you read, what are some ways the believers strengthened and helped one another?

In what ways could generosity and selfless sharing help to create a strong bond between people?

CONNECTING IN COMMUNITY

helps us grow.

How can you better connect with a community so you can receive strength

when you need it and offer help to others when they need it?

_____

_____

_____

_____

_____

_____

_____

_____

_____

_____

_____

_____

_____

_____

_____

Your Biggest Takeaway

Walking Your Walk

Matthew 23:1–12 (NLT)

Then Jesus said to the crowds and to His disciples, "The teachers of religious law and the Pharisees are the official interpreters of the law of Moses. So practice and obey whatever they tell you, but don't follow their example. For they don't practice what they teach. They crush people with unbearable religious demands and never lift a finger to ease the burden.

"Everything they do is for show. On their arms they wear extra wide prayer boxes with Scripture verses inside, and they wear robes with extra long tassels. And they love to sit at the head table at banquets and in the seats of honor in the synagogues. They love to receive respectful greetings as they walk in the marketplaces, and to be called 'Rabbi.'

"Don't let anyone call you 'Rabbi,' for you have only one teacher, and all of you are equal as brothers and sisters. And don't address anyone here on earth as 'Father,' for only God in heaven is your Father. And don't let anyone call you 'Teacher,' for you have only one teacher, the Messiah. The greatest among you must be a servant. But those who exalt themselves will be humbled, and those who humble themselves will be exalted."

Who watches how you live, talk, and act? In other words, who are you a role model to?

How do you think the teachers of religious law and the Pharisees

were setting a bad example for other people?

What does the statement "those who humble themselves will be exalted" mean to you?

Lead by example.

How are you walking your walk—leading and serving others by your example?

In what ways do you need to improve in this area?

_____

_____

_____

_____

_____

_____

_____

_____

_____

_____

_____

_____

_____

_____

_____

A Note From Candace

Living your best life is making sure your walk and talk match. That takes humility—humility to say no to yourself and humility to admit and apologize when your walk and talk don't match. It's bound to happen. We are, after all, only human.

Finding Your Worth

ROMANS 5:1–11 (NLT)

Therefore, since we have been made right in God's sight by faith, we have peace with God because of what Jesus Christ our Lord has done for us. Because of our faith, Christ has brought us into this place of undeserved privilege where we now stand, and we confidently and joyfully look forward to sharing God's glory.

We can rejoice, too, when we run into problems and trials, for we know that they help us develop endurance. And endurance develops strength of character, and character strengthens our confident hope of salvation. And this hope will not lead to disappointment. For we know how dearly God loves us, because He has given us the Holy Spirit to fill our hearts with His love.

When we were utterly helpless, Christ came at just the right time and died for us sinners. Now, most people would not be willing to die for an upright person, though someone might perhaps be willing to die for a person who is especially good. But God showed His great love for us by sending Christ to die for us while we were still sinners. And since we have been made right in God's sight by the blood of Christ, He will certainly save us from God's condemnation. For since our friendship with God was restored by the death of His Son while we were still His enemies, we will certainly be saved through the life of His Son. So now we can rejoice in our wonderful new relationship with God because our Lord Jesus Christ has made us friends of God.

On what do people tend to base their value or worth?

*How easy is it for you to allow your circumstances to affect
your feelings of value or worth? Why?*

How might developing a relationship with God affect a person's self-worth?

God THOUGHT YOU WERE *worth* DYING FOR.

On what do you base your worth? What are some ways you could shift

your focus to what God says about you and your value to Him?

_____

_____

_____

_____

_____

_____

_____

_____

_____

_____

_____

_____

_____

_____

_____

_____

Your Biggest Takeaway

Dare Not to Compare

GALATIANS 6:2–10 (NIV)

Carry each other's burdens, and in this way you will fulfill the law of Christ. If anyone thinks they are something when they are not, they deceive themselves. Each one should test their own actions. Then they can take pride in themselves alone, without comparing themselves to someone else, for each one should carry their own load. Nevertheless, the one who receives instruction in the word should share all good things with their instructor.

Do not be deceived: God cannot be mocked. A man reaps what he sows. Whoever sows to please their flesh, from the flesh will reap destruction; whoever sows to please the Spirit, from the Spirit will reap eternal life. Let us not become weary in doing good, for at the proper time we will reap a harvest if we do not give up. Therefore, as we have opportunity, let us do good to all people, especially to those who belong to the family of believers.

How often do you compare yourself to others?

How do you feel after you compare yourself to someone else?

How might carrying another person's burdens and doing

"good to all people" help you avoid comparing yourself to others?

How do you think comparing ourselves to others can lead to deception?

SEEK ONLY God's approval.

The next time you are tempted to compare yourself to someone,

what are some things you can do instead?

Your Biggest Takeaway

Embracing a Healthy You

I Corinthians 6:12–20 (NLT)

You say, "I am allowed to do anything"—but not everything is good for you. And even though "I am allowed to do anything," I must not become a slave to anything. You say, "Food was made for the stomach, and the stomach for food." (This is true, though someday God will do away with both of them.) But you can't say that our bodies were made for sexual immorality. They were made for the Lord, and the Lord cares about our bodies. And God will raise us from the dead by His power, just as He raised our Lord from the dead.

Don't you realize that your bodies are actually parts of Christ? Should a man take his body, which is part of Christ, and join it to a prostitute? Never! And don't you realize that if a man joins himself to a prostitute, he becomes one body with her? For the Scriptures say, "The two are united into one." But the person who is joined to the Lord is one spirit with Him.

Run from sexual sin! No other sin so clearly affects the body as this one does. For sexual immorality is a sin against your own body. Don't you realize that your body is the temple of the Holy Spirit, who lives in you and was given to you by God? You do not belong to yourself, for God bought you with a high price. So you must honor God with your body.

How well are you caring for yourself physically, emotionally, mentally, and spiritually?

In what ways might people dishonor God with their bodies?

In what ways might people honor Him with their bodies?

What temptations that could lead to an unhealthy lifestyle

do you struggle with and need to run from?

WHEN YOU EMBRACE
A HEALTHY LIFESTYLE,
YOU HONOR

God

WITH

your body.

What are some practical steps you can take in the coming week to embrace a healthier you?

_____

_____

_____

_____

_____

_____

_____

_____

_____

_____

_____

_____

_____

_____

_____

_____

_____

A Note From Candace

Let's face it: our bodies want what they want, even when we know it's not good. If you find yourself struggling here, find a friend who will help you stay accountable. Temptation is easier to resist when someone is walking alongside you.

One Day at a Time

Matthew 6:25–34 (NLT)

"That is why I tell you not to worry about everyday life—whether you have enough food and drink, or enough clothes to wear. Isn't life more than food, and your body more than clothing? Look at the birds. They don't plant or harvest or store food in barns, for your heavenly Father feeds them. And aren't you far more valuable to Him than they are? Can all your worries add a single moment to your life? And why worry about your clothing? Look at the lilies of the field and how they grow. They don't work or make their clothing, yet Solomon in all his glory was not dressed as beautifully as they are. And if God cares so wonderfully for wildflowers that are here today and thrown into the fire tomorrow, He will certainly care for you. Why do you have so little faith? So don't worry about these things, saying, 'What will we eat? What will we drink? What will we wear?' These things dominate the thoughts of unbelievers, but your heavenly Father already knows all your needs. Seek the Kingdom of God above all else, and live righteously, and He will give you everything you need. So don't worry about tomorrow, for tomorrow will bring its own worries. Today's trouble is enough for today."

What things in life—big or little—tend to cause you the most anxiety?

How does God's care for us compare to how He cares for birds and flowers?

In these verses, what does Jesus say we should do instead of worry?

YOUR NEEDS

matter to

God.

What needs do you have in your life right now?

If you'd like, write a prayer, asking God to meet each need.

_____

_____

_____

_____

_____

_____

_____

_____

_____

_____

_____

_____

_____

_____

_____

_____

_____

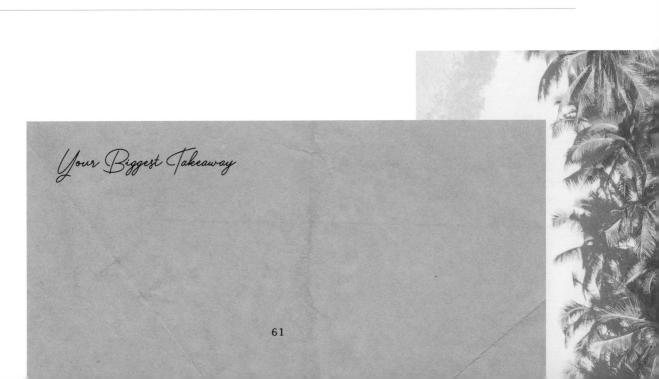

Your Biggest Takeaway

Balancing It All

ECCLESIASTES 3:1–8 (ESV)

For everything there is a season, and a time for every matter under heaven:

a time to be born, and a time to die;

a time to plant, and a time to pluck up what is planted;

a time to kill, and a time to heal;

a time to break down, and a time to build up;

a time to weep, and a time to laugh;

a time to mourn, and a time to dance;

a time to cast away stones, and a time to gather stones together;

a time to embrace, and a time to refrain from embracing;

a time to seek, and a time to lose;

a time to keep, and a time to cast away;

a time to tear, and a time to sew;

a time to keep silence, and a time to speak;

a time to love, and a time to hate;

a time for war, and a time for peace.

What things are you trying to balance or juggle in your life right now?

Which of these verses do you most relate to? Why?

How do these verses help you think differently about balancing everything in your life?

THERE IS FREEDOM IN

letting go

OF

perfection.

What things do you need to let go of to maintain better balance in your life?

How can you start letting go of trying to do everything perfectly?

A Note From Candace

You *can* do it all . . . just not all at once. Seriously, life is lived in seasons. Life ebbs and flows. Sink into the season you are in, enjoy it, learn all you can, and rest assured that the next season is right around the corner.

Life Is Unpredictable

JOB 1:13–22 (NLT)

One day when Job's sons and daughters were feasting at the oldest brother's house, a messenger arrived at Job's home with this news: "Your oxen were plowing, with the donkeys feeding beside them, when the Sabeans raided us. They stole all the animals and killed all the farmhands. I am the only one who escaped to tell you.". . .

While he was still speaking, another messenger arrived with this news: "Your sons and daughters were feasting in their oldest brother's home. Suddenly, a powerful wind swept in from the wilderness and hit the house on all sides. The house collapsed, and all your children are dead. I am the only one who escaped to tell you."

Job stood up and tore his robe in grief. Then he shaved his head and fell to the ground to worship. He said, "I came naked from my mother's womb, and I will be naked when I leave. The LORD gave me what I had, and the LORD has taken it away. Praise the name of the LORD!"

In all of this, Job did not sin by blaming God.

What unpredictable loss have you experienced in your life?

Though full of grief, Job responded to his incredible loss by praising God's name.

How do you typically respond to suffering in your life?

How easy is it for you to blame God or other people

for difficult circumstances in your life? Why?

ALTHOUGH LIFE IS UNPREDICTABLE, *God* REMAINS THE *same.*

What can you learn from Job about responding to unpredictable circumstances in your life?

_____

_____

_____

_____

_____

_____

_____

_____

_____

_____

_____

_____

_____

_____

_____

_____

Your Biggest Takeaway

Self-Control

GENESIS 39:2–12 (ESV)

The LORD was with Joseph, and he became a successful man, and he was in the house of his Egyptian master. His master saw that the LORD was with him and that the LORD caused all that he did to succeed in his hands. So Joseph found favor in his sight and attended him, and he made him overseer of his house and put him in charge of all that he had. . . .

Now Joseph was handsome in form and appearance. And after a time his master's wife cast her eyes on Joseph and said, "Lie with me." But he refused and said to his master's wife, "Behold, because of me my master has no concern about anything in the house, and he has put everything that he has in my charge. He is not greater in this house than I am, nor has he kept back anything from me except you, because you are his wife. How then can I do this great wickedness and sin against God?" And as she spoke to Joseph day after day, he would not listen to her, to lie beside her or to be with her.

But one day, when he went into the house to do his work and none of the men of the house was there in the house, she caught him by his garment, saying, "Lie with me." But he left his garment in her hand and fled and got out of the house.

When is self-control easy for you? When is it hard?

How was Joseph's self-control tested in these verses?

Based on these verses from Genesis, how would you describe Joseph's character?

Self-control begins by *submitting* ourselves to *God.*

How does Joseph's example of self-control inspire you?

In what areas of your life do you want to develop better self-control?

Your Biggest Takeaway

The Power of Grace

I Peter 3:8–16 (NIV)

Finally, all of you, be like-minded, be sympathetic, love one another, be compassionate and humble. Do not repay evil with evil or insult with insult. On the contrary, repay evil with blessing, because to this you were called so that you may inherit a blessing. For,

> "Whoever would love life
>   and see good days
> must keep their tongue from evil
>   and their lips from deceitful speech.
> They must turn from evil and do good;
>   they must seek peace and pursue it.
> For the eyes of the Lord are on the righteous
>   and His ears are attentive to their prayer,
> but the face of the Lord is against those who do evil."

Who is going to harm you if you are eager to do good? But even if you should suffer for what is right, you are blessed. "Do not fear their threats; do not be frightened." But in your hearts revere Christ as Lord. Always be prepared to give an answer to everyone who asks you to give the reason for the hope that you have. But do this with gentleness and respect, keeping a clear conscience, so that those who speak maliciously against your good behavior in Christ may be ashamed of their slander.

When you feel criticized or rejected, how do you usually respond?

How difficult is it for you to show kindness to someone

who has treated you badly or insulted you?

Based on these verses, how do you think God wants us to respond when we are mistreated?

God's grace

EMPOWERS US TO DO WHAT WE CAN'T DO ON

our own.

How can you respond with grace the next time you are criticized? If you'd like, write a prayer, asking God to give you the grace to respond in kindness to people who lash out at you or hurt you.

Consistency
Matters

DANIEL 6:3–10 (CSB)

Daniel distinguished himself above the administrators and satraps because he had an extraordinary spirit, so the king planned to set him over the whole realm. The administrators and satraps, therefore, kept trying to find a charge against Daniel regarding the kingdom. But they could find no charge or corruption, for he was trustworthy, and no negligence or corruption was found in him. Then these men said, "We will never find any charge against this Daniel unless we find something against him concerning the law of his God."

So the administrators and satraps went together to the king and said to him, "May King Darius live forever. All the administrators of the kingdom, the prefects, satraps, advisers, and governors have agreed that the king should establish an ordinance and enforce an edict that for thirty days, anyone who petitions any god or man except you, the king, will be thrown into the lions' den. Therefore, Your Majesty, establish the edict and sign the document so that, as a law of the Medes and Persians, it is irrevocable and cannot be changed." So King Darius signed the written edict.

When Daniel learned that the document had been signed, he went into his house. The windows in its upstairs room opened toward Jerusalem, and three times a day he got down on his knees, prayed, and gave thanks to his God, just as he had done before.

How consistent are you in spending time with God—

whether through praying or reading the Bible?

How would you describe Daniel's character from these verses?

What can you learn and put into practice from Daniel's relationship with God?

Prayer

IS THE LINK THAT CONNECTS US WITH

God.

— A. B. SIMPSON

In which areas do you need to be more consistent in your relationship with God?

What practical steps can you take to more consistently spend time with Him this week?

_____

_____

_____

_____

_____

_____

_____

_____

_____

_____

_____

_____

_____

_____

_____

_____

Your Biggest Takeaway

The Art of Authenticity

I John 2:1–11 (NLT)

My dear children, I am writing this to you so that you will not sin. But if anyone does sin, we have an advocate who pleads our case before the Father. He is Jesus Christ, the One who is truly righteous. He Himself is the sacrifice that atones for our sins—and not only our sins but the sins of all the world.

And we can be sure that we know Him if we obey His commandments. If someone claims, "I know God," but doesn't obey God's commandments, that person is a liar and is not living in the truth. But those who obey God's word truly show how completely they love Him. That is how we know we are living in Him. Those who say they live in God should live their lives as Jesus did.

Dear friends, I am not writing a new commandment for you; rather it is an old one you have had from the very beginning. This old commandment— to love one another—is the same message you heard before. Yet it is also new. Jesus lived the truth of this commandment, and you also are living it. For the darkness is disappearing, and the true light is already shining.

If anyone claims, "I am living in the light," but hates a fellow believer, that person is still living in darkness. Anyone who loves a fellow believer is living in the light and does not cause others to stumble. But anyone who hates a fellow believer is still living and walking in darkness. Such a person does not know the way to go, having been blinded by the darkness.

How would you describe your relationship with God?

Based on these verses, what do you think it means to live authentically as a follower of Jesus?

Describe how you are living in the light or walking in the darkness.

Live YOUR LIFE AS Jesus did.

How do these verses specifically encourage you to love other people as Jesus loves them?

What changes can you make this week to live a more authentic lifestyle?

_____
_____
_____
_____
_____
_____
_____
_____
_____
_____
_____
_____
_____
_____
_____
_____
_____
_____

Your Biggest Takeaway

Abundant Living

Psalm 16 (NASB)

Preserve me, O God, for I take refuge in You.

I said to the Lord, "You are my Lord;

I have no good besides You." . . .

The Lord is the portion of my inheritance and my cup;

You support my lot.

The lines have fallen to me in pleasant places;

Indeed, my heritage is beautiful to me.

I will bless the Lord who has counseled me;

Indeed, my mind instructs me in the night.

I have set the Lord continually before me;

Because He is at my right hand, I will not be shaken.

Therefore my heart is glad and my glory rejoices;

My flesh also will dwell securely.

For You will not abandon my soul to Sheol;

Nor will You allow Your Holy One to undergo decay.

You will make known to me the path of life;

In Your presence is fullness of joy;

In Your right hand there are pleasures forever.

What or who makes you feel the safest in your life?

How would you describe David's attitude toward God when he wrote this psalm?

What part of this psalm do you find most comforting? Why?

TRUSTING *God* COMPLETELY IS THE FIRST STEP TOWARD *abundant living.*

In which areas of your life do you need to experience "abundant living"?

How can you trust God more fully for His abundance in your life?

A Note From Candace

To be safe, to have a place of refuge, to be full, to be guided, to be loved greatly . . . this is the abundant life. Abundant living can be found only in Jesus.

Heavenly Wisdom

Proverbs 3:13; James 3:13–18 (NLT)

Joyful is the person who finds wisdom, the one who gains understanding.

If you are wise and understand God's ways, prove it by living an honorable life, doing good works with the humility that comes from wisdom. But if you are bitterly jealous and there is selfish ambition in your heart, don't cover up the truth with boasting and lying. For jealousy and selfishness are not God's kind of wisdom. Such things are earthly, unspiritual, and demonic. For wherever there is jealousy and selfish ambition, there you will find disorder and evil of every kind.

But the wisdom from above is first of all pure. It is also peace loving, gentle at all times, and willing to yield to others. It is full of mercy and the fruit of good deeds. It shows no favoritism and is always sincere. And those who are peacemakers will plant seeds of peace and reap a harvest of righteousness.

When you need wisdom, who do you talk to or what do you do?

How would you define wisdom based on these verses?

What are some of the differences between heavenly wisdom and earthly wisdom?

EARTHLY WISDOM IS DOING
WHAT COMES NATURALLY.
GODLY WISDOM IS DOING
WHAT THE

Holy

Spirit

COMPELS US TO DO.

— CHARLES STANLEY

In what areas of your life are you in need of wisdom to live more honorably, peacefully, mercifully, or sincerely? If you'd like, write a prayer, asking God for His wisdom in these areas.

Your Biggest Takeaway

A Humble Heart

PHILIPPIANS 2:1–11 (NASB)

Therefore if there is any encouragement in Christ, if there is any consolation of love, if there is any fellowship of the Spirit, if any affection and compassion, make my joy complete by being of the same mind, maintaining the same love, united in spirit, intent on one purpose. Do nothing from selfishness or empty conceit, but with humility of mind regard one another as more important than yourselves; do not merely look out for your own personal interests, but also for the interests of others. Have this attitude in yourselves which was also in Christ Jesus, who, although He existed in the form of God, did not regard equality with God a thing to be grasped, but emptied Himself, taking the form of a bond-servant, and being made in the likeness of men. Being found in appearance as a man, He humbled Himself by becoming obedient to the point of death, even death on a cross. For this reason also, God highly exalted Him, and bestowed on Him the name which is above every name, so that at the name of Jesus EVERY KNEE WILL BOW, of those who are in heaven and on earth and under the earth, and that every tongue will confess that Jesus Christ is Lord, to the glory of God the Father.

Who is the humblest person you know? What makes this person so humble?

In what ways did Jesus demonstrate humility as described in these verses?

According to these verses, how can we demonstrate humility in our relationships with others?

Humility

STARTS IN THE

heart

AND EXPRESSES
ITSELF IN THE
ATTITUDE AND
ACTIONS.

In which areas do you need to grow in humility?

What are some practical steps you can take to develop a humble attitude?

_____

_____

_____

_____

_____

_____

_____

_____

_____

_____

_____

_____

_____

_____

_____

_____

Your Biggest Takeaway

Using Your Words

James 3:1–12 (NIV)

Not many of you should become teachers, my fellow believers, because you know that we who teach will be judged more strictly. We all stumble in many ways. Anyone who is never at fault in what they say is perfect, able to keep their whole body in check.

When we put bits into the mouths of horses to make them obey us, we can turn the whole animal. Or take ships as an example. Although they are so large and are driven by strong winds, they are steered by a very small rudder wherever the pilot wants to go. Likewise, the tongue is a small part of the body, but it makes great boasts. Consider what a great forest is set on fire by a small spark. The tongue also is a fire, a world of evil among the parts of the body. It corrupts the whole body, sets the whole course of one's life on fire, and is itself set on fire by hell.

All kinds of animals, birds, reptiles and sea creatures are being tamed and have been tamed by mankind, but no human being can tame the tongue. It is a restless evil, full of deadly poison.

With the tongue we praise our Lord and Father, and with it we curse human beings, who have been made in God's likeness. Out of the same mouth come praise and cursing. My brothers and sisters, this should not be. Can both fresh water and salt water flow from the same spring? My brothers and sisters, can a fig tree bear olives, or a grapevine bear figs? Neither can a salt spring produce fresh water.

When have others' words hurt you? When have others' words helped you?

How can one word be like a spark that starts a forest fire?

The verses contain several different examples from nature to describe the power of our words.

Which one do you relate to most and why?

WORDS CAN HEAL OR HURT.

Choose

YOUR WORDS

wisely.

How can you use your words to bring hope, life, and encouragement to others?

How can you honor God and others with your words?

A Note From Candace

Words have power. Power to build up and power to tear down. Sometimes I wish I could reel back in the words I just said. Ugh. Slowing down is key. Listen first, think, and then speak.

Honest Living

EPHESIANS 4:22—32 (NIV)

You were taught, with regard to your former way of life, to put off your old self, which is being corrupted by its deceitful desires; to be made new in the attitude of your minds; and to put on the new self, created to be like God in true righteousness and holiness.

Therefore each of you must put off falsehood and speak truthfully to your neighbor, for we are all members of one body. "In your anger do not sin": Do not let the sun go down while you are still angry, and do not give the devil a foothold. Anyone who has been stealing must steal no longer, but must work, doing something useful with their own hands, that they may have something to share with those in need.

Do not let any unwholesome talk come out of your mouths, but only what is helpful for building others up according to their needs, that it may benefit those who listen. And do not grieve the Holy Spirit of God, with whom you were sealed for the day of redemption. Get rid of all bitterness, rage and anger, brawling and slander, along with every form of malice. Be kind and compassionate to one another, forgiving each other, just as in Christ God forgave you.

Do you think it's difficult to live honestly in today's society? Why or why not?

The verses you just read contain lots of practical examples and advice. Which is the most meaningful to you?

In what ways do you think our "new self" should be different from our "old self"?

BUILD
others up
WITH YOUR
words.

What are some practical steps you can take toward honest

living that will honor God and inspire others?

_____

_____

_____

_____

_____

_____

_____

_____

_____

_____

_____

_____

_____

_____

Your Biggest Takeaway

Growing in Compassion

PSALM 103:6–13 (NASB)

The LORD performs righteous deeds

And judgments for all who are oppressed.

He made known His ways to Moses,

His acts to the sons of Israel.

The LORD is compassionate and gracious,

Slow to anger and abounding in lovingkindness.

He will not always strive with us,

Nor will He keep His anger forever.

He has not dealt with us according to our sins,

Nor rewarded us according to our iniquities.

For as high as the heavens are above the earth,

So great is His lovingkindness toward those who fear Him.

As far as the east is from the west,

So far has He removed our transgressions from us.

Just as a father has compassion on his children,

So the LORD has compassion on those who fear Him.

What is the most compassionate act you've personally witnessed or experienced?

According to David, the author of Psalm 103,

what are some of the ways God shows compassion to His people?

How have you experienced God's compassion?

How have you shown similar compassion toward another person?

THE FRUIT OF LOVE
IS SERVICE, WHICH IS

compassion

IN
action.

— MOTHER TERESA

What are some changes you can make or actions you can take in

your life so you can live more compassionately?

_____

_____

_____

_____

_____

_____

_____

_____

_____

_____

_____

_____

_____

_____

_____

Your Biggest Takeaway

Stay True to Yourself

ROMANS 14:1–10 (CSB)

Accept anyone who is weak in faith, but don't argue about disputed matters. One person believes he may eat anything, while one who is weak eats only vegetables. One who eats must not look down on one who does not eat, and one who does not eat must not judge one who does, because God has accepted him. Who are you to judge another's household servant? Before his own Lord he stands or falls. And he will stand, because the Lord is able to make him stand.

One person judges one day to be more important than another day. Someone else judges every day to be the same. Let each one be fully convinced in his own mind. Whoever observes the day, observes it for the honor of the Lord. Whoever eats, eats for the Lord, since he gives thanks to God; and whoever does not eat, it is for the Lord that he does not eat it, and he gives thanks to God. For none of us lives for himself, and no one dies for himself. If we live, we live for the Lord; and if we die, we die for the Lord. Therefore, whether we live or die, we belong to the Lord. Christ died and returned to life for this: that He might be Lord over both the dead and the living. But you, why do you judge your brother or sister? Or you, why do you despise your brother or sister? For we will all stand before the judgment seat of God.

What kinds of expectations do other people place on you?

How does this make you feel?

What are some of the "disputed matters" that people tend to argue

about concerning expectations of how a person should live for God?

(Example: People might disagree about what is acceptable for a follower of Jesus to wear or eat.)

"If we live, we live for the Lord; and if we die, we die for the Lord."

What do these words mean for you in how you should live your life?

YOU

belong

TO

Jesus.

How can you remain true to yourself—that is, true to who God made

you to be—even when others put their expectations on you?

A Note From Candace

As an actress I perform for an audience. In my real life, I have an audience too. An audience of One—Jesus. So when the critics come, and they come for all of us, remember you are playing to an audience of One and only One—Jesus.